Just One Fool Thing
After Another

A full line of western books is available
from Gibbs Smith, Publisher.
Other books in this series are:

Don't Squat With Yer Spurs On!
A Cowboy's Guide to Life
by Texas Bix Bender

**Never Ask a Man
the Size of His Spread**
A Cowgirl's Guide to Life
by Gladiola Montana

Laughing Stock
A Cow's Guide to Life
by Texas Bix Bender

Just One Fool Thing After Another

A Cowfolks' Guide to Romance

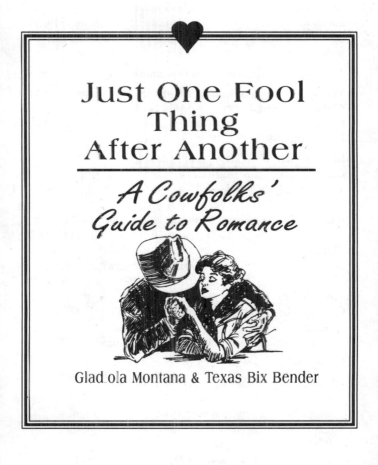

Gladiola Montana & Texas Bix Bender

GIBBS·SMITH
P
PUBLISHER

97 96 95   10 9 8 7 6 5

The quotations in this book come from a mixture of lore and experience.

This is a Peregrine Smith Book, published by
Gibbs Smith, Publisher
P.O. Box 667
Layton, Utah 84041

Design by **Mary Ellen Thompson,** TTA Design
Illustrations by **Bonnie Cazier,** © 1994 by Gibbs Smith, Publisher: 4, 6,
10, 14, 20, 22, 28, 30, 34, 36, 38, 44, 46, 52, 60, 62, 70, 78, 82, 84, 90,
94, 102, 106, 112, 118, 124, 132, 134, 136, 142
Illustrations by **Steve Egan,** ©1994 by Gibbs Smith, Publisher:
Animation, 12, 18, 26, 40, 56, 66, 68, 76, 88, 100, 110, 114, 122, 128,
138, 144
Illustrations by **Jeff Gore,** © 1994 by Gibbs Smith, Publisher: 8, 16, 24,
32, 42, 48, 50, 54, 58, 64, 72, 80, 86, 92, 96, 98, 104, 108, 116, 120,
126, 130, 140
Cover dancing couple by Richard Haight, © 1993 by Gibbs Smith,
Publisher
Cover background courtesy Tandy Leather Company, Roy, UT

Printed and bound in the U.S.A.

Library of Congress Cataloging-in Publication Data
Bender Texas Bix, 1949
  Just one fool thing after another: a cowfolks' guide to romance /
  by Texas Bix Bender and Gladiola Montana.
    ISBN 0-87905-595-2 (pbk.)
    1. Love–Humor. 2. Cowboys–Humor 3. Cowgirls– Humor.
I. Montana, Gladiola. II. Title.
PN6231.L6B46 1994
818'.5402–dc20   93-47139
                                                         CIP

There's no cure
for lovesickness,
and nobody
really wants one.

Sometimes flowers
don't say it very well;
you need to explain yourself.

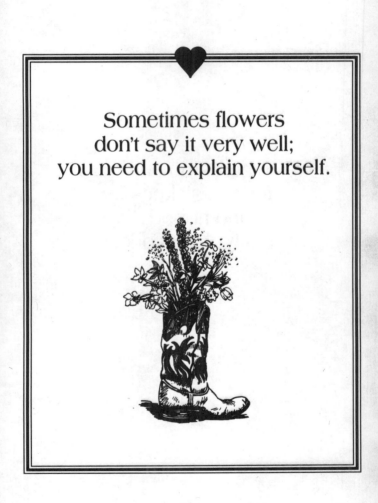

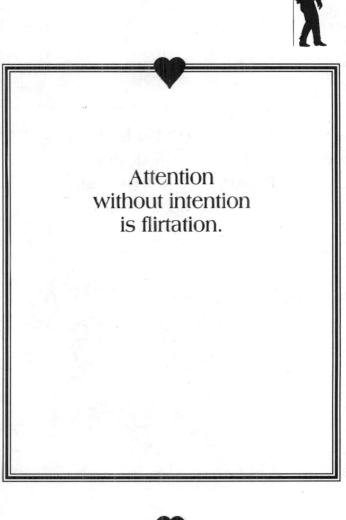

Attention
without intention
is flirtation.

When you go fishin'
for compliments,
make sure you're usin'
the right bait.

If you're in doubt
about whether to
kiss somebody,
give 'em the benefit
of the doubt.

No matter how much
you trust your horse,
you'd be foolish not
to hitch 'er in town.

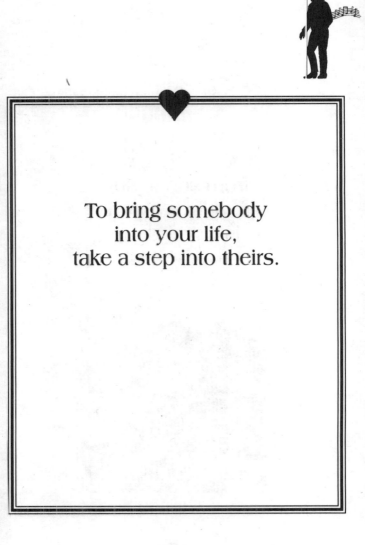

To bring somebody
into your life,
take a step into theirs.

The ranch is work
from sun to sun,
but love's work
is never done.

A wagonload of nursin'
don't amount to
a spoonful of sweeteartin'.

If your mind's set to ride
a buckin' bronc,
you'd better be prepared
for the bruises.

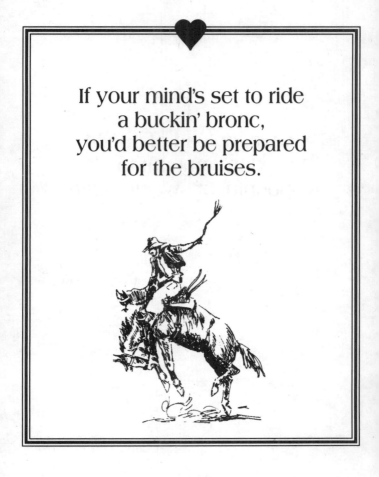

In all the history of the world,
there was only
one indispensable man
and one indispensable woman.

When you fall into
somebody's arms,
you're fallin'
into their hands as well.

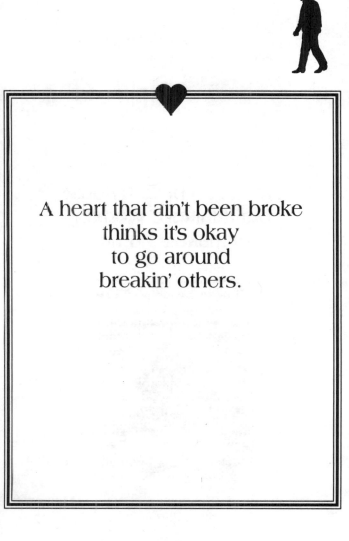

A heart that ain't been broke
thinks it's okay
to go around
breakin' others.

A man can build a house,
but it takes a woman
to make it home.

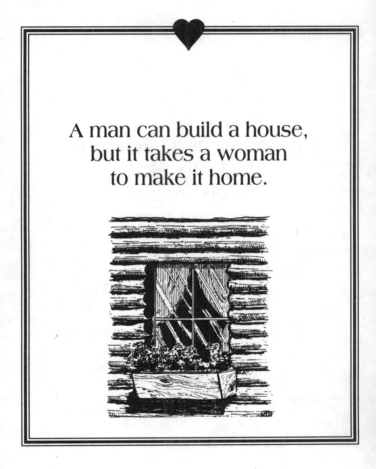

If you wanta stay single,
look for a perfect mate.

Don't let a fool kiss you,
or a kiss fool you.

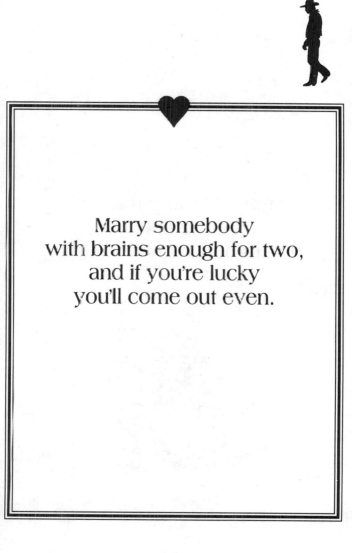

Marry somebody
with brains enough for two,
and if you're lucky
you'll come out even.

It may be more romantic
to be the first love,
but it's better to be the last.

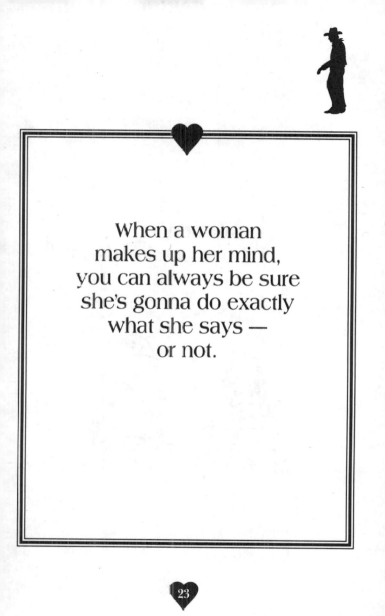

When a woman
makes up her mind,
you can always be sure
she's gonna do exactly
what she says —
or not.

Women flirt
to be appreciated;
men mean it.

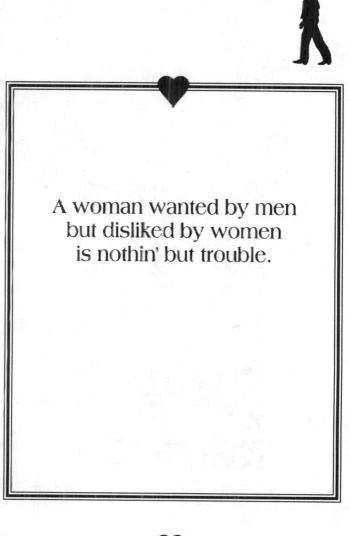

A woman wanted by men
but disliked by women
is nothin' but trouble.

When you go to town, go together.

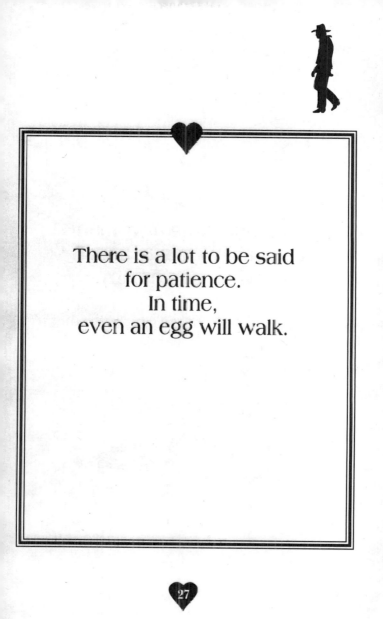

There is a lot to be said
for patience.
In time,
even an egg will walk.

The only time a woman
can easily change a man
is when he's a baby.

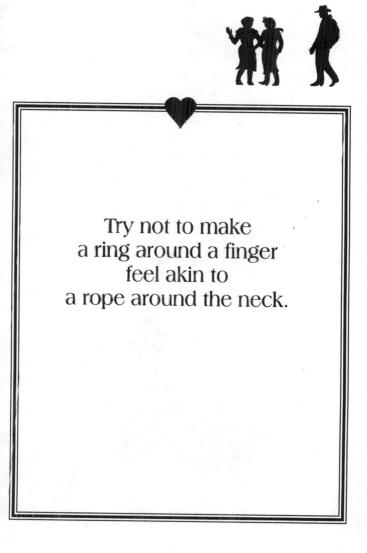

Try not to make
a ring around a finger
feel akin to
a rope around the neck.

It's a lot cheaper
to borrow money
than to marry for it.

To love and win
is the best thing.
To love and lose
is the next best.

It's great to ride together,
work together,
and come home exhausted
together at the end of the day.

Be quick to mend fences.

Never go to bed mad.
Stay up and fight it out.

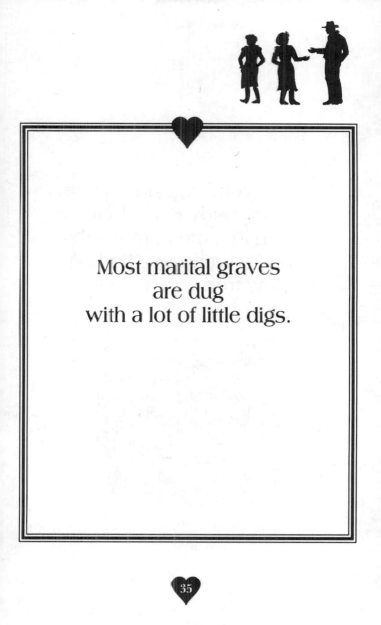

Most marital graves
are dug
with a lot of little digs.

When you're pickin' flowers
everybody gets along.
When it's time to muck the
stalls is when you find out
how true your love is.

Just because
you don't see tears
on the outside,
don't mean it ain't
pourin' on the inside.

No matter how much
he loves you,
sometimes he'd just rather
have an inch of rain
than anything else in the world.

Stolen kisses
require an accomplice.

Love is a rocky trail,
but it promises a scenic ride.

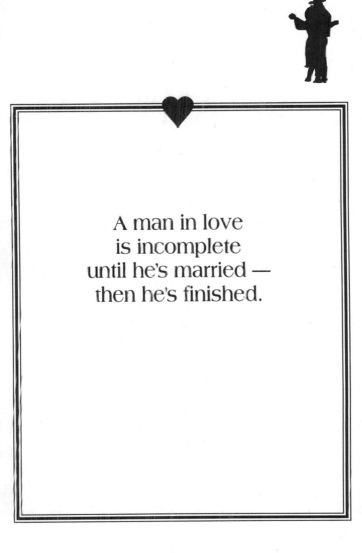

A man in love
is incomplete
until he's married —
then he's finished.

Pullin' your hair out
over a broken heart
will only make you bald.

If women are foolish,
it's because
the good Lord made 'em
a match for men.

A good woman
won't take a man's gift
less'n she'll take
the man as well.

Faults are thick
when love is thin.

For better or for worse
means for good.

When you don't have a thing in
the world to worry about,
you go and get married,
and suddenly the world is
a worrisome place.

Embers are easily rekindled,
but ashes leave no hope.

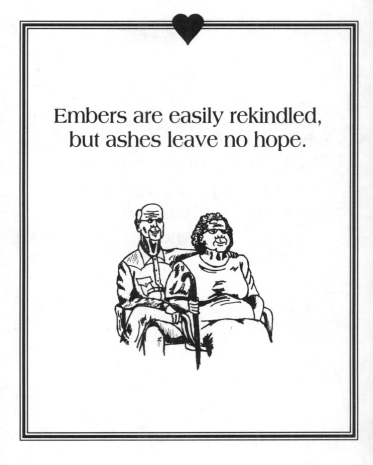

When you can't keep
anything from 'em,
you love 'em.

Romance looks great
comin' and goin'.

If you've got
love in your heart,
you've got
spurs in your sides.

Horse sense
and affairs of the heart
are an unusual pair.

Never spur
a willing horse.

When there are
two on a horse,
one must ride behind.

Some women
think the best way
to tell a good man
or a good watermelon
is to give 'em a good thump.

When a man asks a woman
to share his lot,
she has a right
to know how big it is.

You gotta wear the boot
to know where it pinches.

Don't wait
to know somebody better
to kiss 'em.
Kiss 'em and you'll
know 'em better.

Don't get involved
with anyone
whose wishbone is stronger
than their backbone.

Men react to specific needs.
Women seldom have them.

The ties of marriage
are not slip knots.

Big problems
will pull you together.
It's the little things
that tear you apart.

Never kiss a fool —
more'n once.

63

The best way
to get married
is with ignorance
and confidence.

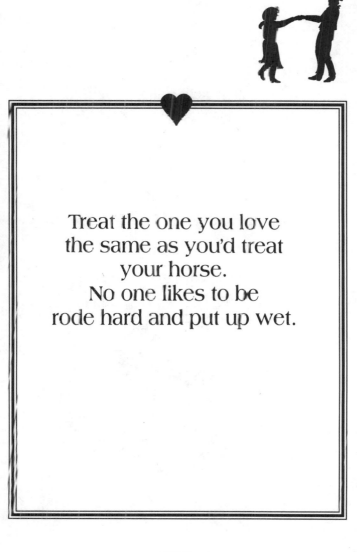

Treat the one you love
the same as you'd treat
your horse.
No one likes to be
rode hard and put up wet.

Never use a knife
to cut a tender connection.

Bad habits
are the barbed wire
of romance;
they can
wear the hide off it.

Just because you learned a lot
from your last lover's leap,
don't mean you ain't jumpin' off
a different cliff this time.

Once her broken heart mends,
a woman usually
feels like a new man.

When you start to
feelin' sorry for yourself,
remember that
whoever has to live with you
has a lot more
to feel sorry about.

Man is straw;
woman is fire.
When the devil blows,
it's hell.

If you're gonna leave,
leave while you're
still lookin' good.

Bein' on a diet
don't mean you can't look
at the menu.
Just don't make a selection.

Lust is like a prairie rose:
it lasts while it lasts.

Don't waste your time
lovin' somebody
you can't laugh with.

Wild oats
can lead to
a sad harvest.

When the horse dies,
get off.

A good man's smile
is worth a million winks
from a bar hopper.

Women don't make
fools out of men;
they just give 'em
the opportunity.

If somethin' happens to your pardner and you don't know their business, you're in for a big surprise and a long ride.

Don't waste time
on someone
you can easily
run the whole length of.

Being a friend to somebody
you'd rather be in love with,
is like being invited behind
the barn to look at the stars
and just lookin' at the stars.

Never make a promise
without some idea
of how you're gonna keep it.

Love from afar
is too far off
to do you any good.

In the spring,
if your fancy turns
to the opposite sex,
you've been wastin' the winter.

Never marry a widow
whose first husband
was poisoned.

Remember,
when an argument's over,
it's done.
You'd be plum loco
to start it up again.

Marriage is like a fiddle:
the strings are there
whether the music's playin'
or not.

The best way for a woman
to look ten years younger
is to get rid of
the old fart she sleeps with.

When your sweetheart
wants a long talk,
you'd better be willin'
for a long listen.

Love is a fire
you can't buy insurance for.

Sometimes,
what you're lookin' forward to
is exactly what
you should be watchin' out for.

The best way to reach
the heights of romance
is to stay on the level.

If a woman looks old,
she is old; if she looks young,
she is young; if she looks back,
follow her.

Lovin' somebody
for all they're worth
ain't quite the same as
lovin' somebody
for all you're worth.

The best way
to get around somebody
is to hug 'em.

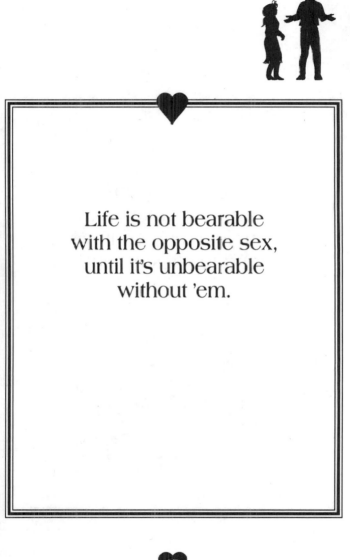

Life is not bearable
with the opposite sex,
until it's unbearable
without 'em.

Looks may last
and they may not,
but love and courage
tend to stick around.

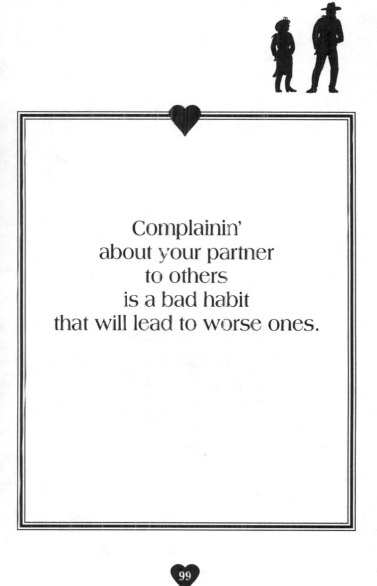

Complainin'
about your partner
to others
is a bad habit
that will lead to worse ones.

A stone stops rollin'
when it lands near
the kinda moss
it's been lookin' to gather.

It's best not to chew
on somethin'
that's eatin' you.

If you gotta grab a hold of your mate to tell 'em somethin', best thing to do is grab a hold of your tongue instead.

When the skillet's sizzlin',
somethin's cookin'.

Never go quietly;
always raise hell about it.

Don't let your
sweetheart's old flame
burn you up.

You gotta get a hold of yourself before you can get a hold
on a good marriage.

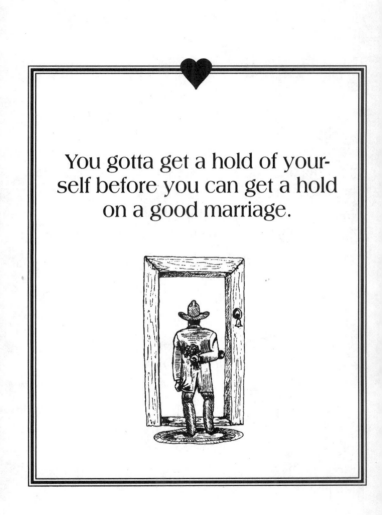

Love is just
one fool thing
after another.

A big heart
is better than
a big house.

Sayin' what you please
only as long as
you please somebody,
ain't sayin' what you please.

Approach love
like a bowl of chili:
the hotter the better.

Don't
measure each other
in inches.

To appreciate love,
you have to know
you can lose it.

When a man and a woman
first get married,
they tell each other everything.
After a while,
they know without tellin'.

Don't share your blanket
if you don't intend
to share your heart.

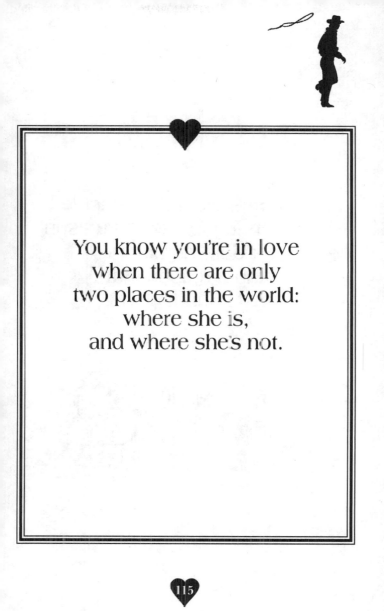

You know you're in love
when there are only
two places in the world:
where she is,
and where she's not.

There's a big difference
between a good sound reason
for doin' somethin',
and a reason that
just sounds good.

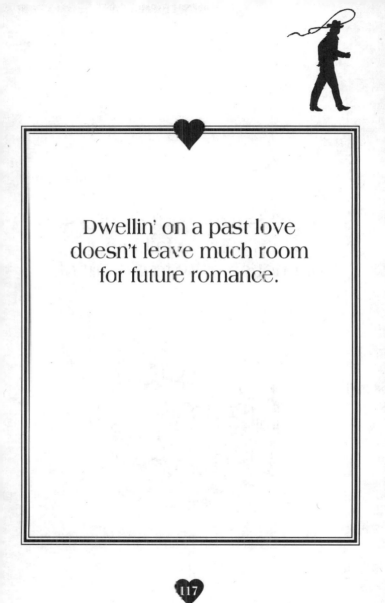

Dwellin' on a past love
doesn't leave much room
for future romance.

Love is like a soft mattress:
it's easy to fall into,
but not so easy to get out of.

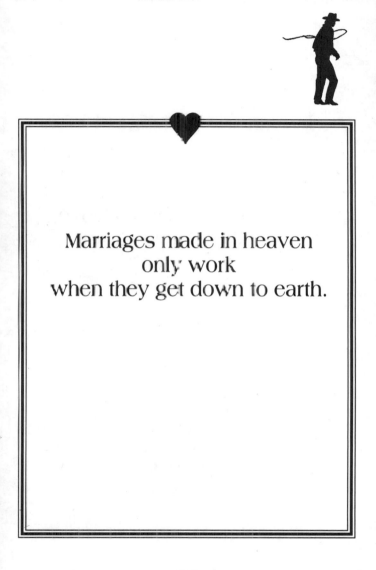

Marriages made in heaven
only work
when they get down to earth.

Look after the one you love,
and the one you love
will look after you.

Don't be surprised
if a vision the night before
is a sight in the mornin'.

It's a dead-end canyon
to dwell on a love
that mighta been.

If you can't stand the heat,
get out of the bedroom.

If you want to
grow old gracefully,
don't try to learn new dances.

Women have to
be in the mood.
Men just have to
be in the room.

The best way
to cure a pain in the behind
is to kiss 'em goodbye.

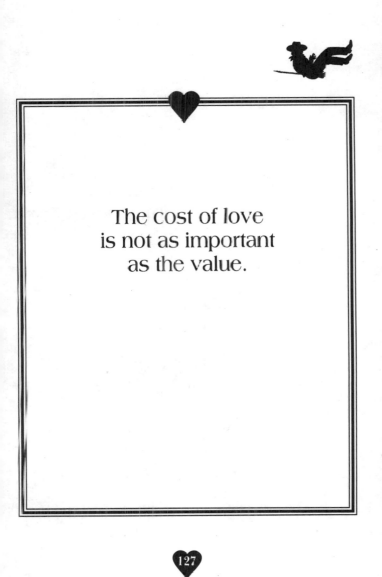

The cost of love
is not as important
as the value.

Be sure the goin' up
is worth the comin' down.

Love fills you
with the
strong breath of livin'.

If you don't quarrel
once in a while,
one of you is just dumb.

As you get more experienced
in romantic matters,
you'll not only know more,
you'll know better.

A nag is a drag
on any love affair.

It is better
to be a widower's
second wife
than his first.

A day without a shared laugh is a sorry day.

There are two things
a man must do
to keep his wife happy.
First, let her think
she's gettin' her way.
Second, let her have it.

The art of horse sitting
and the art of marriage
are easily acquired
if you keep at 'em
from dawn to dusk,
day in, day out.

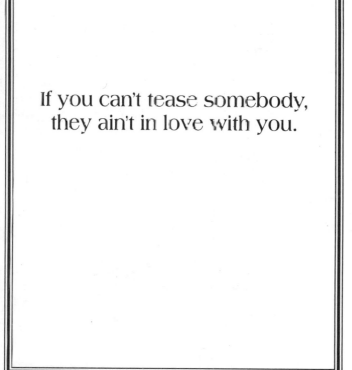

If you can't tease somebody,
they ain't in love with you.

Don't go puttin' up a gate
to someone's heart
'til you've got a
corral around it.

A man who wears
two faces under one hat
is not to be trusted.

Among other drawbacks,
if you live alone
you'll never know if you
snore.

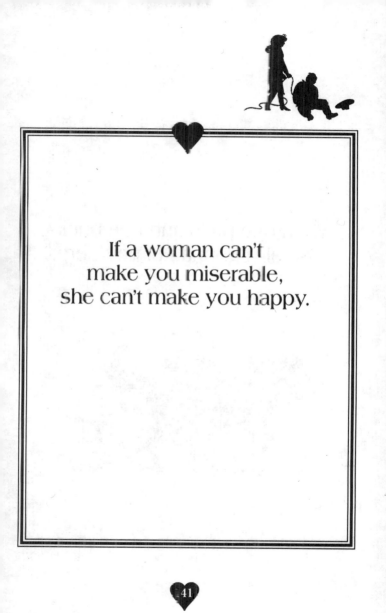

If a woman can't
make you miserable,
she can't make you happy.

When one pulls and one bucks,
you ain't gonna get nowhere.

You never realize
how long a day is
until you lose your heart.

Remember,
somebody nice
to come home to
is somebody nice
to go out with, too.